GW00694074

SUNBIRD
PUBLISHING

First published 2003
2 4 6 8 10 9 7 5 3 1
Sunbird Publishing (Pty) Ltd
34 Sunset Avenue, Llandudno, Cape Town, South Africa
Registration number: 4850177827

Publisher Dick Wilkins
Editor Brenda Brickman
Designer Mandy McKay
Production Manager Andrew de Kock

Reproduction by Unifoto (Pty) Ltd, Cape Town
Printed and bound by Tien Wah Press (Pte) Ltd, Singapore

ISBN 0 624 04079 8

TITLE PAGE Dense stands of a variety of Namaqua daisies at Kamieskroon, Namaqualand, during spring. Seeds of the annuals lie dormant during the hot, dry summer months, germinating after good autumn rains, and bursting into bloom after sufficient winter rainfall. The resulting carpet of flowers acts as an advertisement for insect pollinators. Most prominent here are orange Namaqualand daisy (*Dimorphotheca sinuata*), berggousblom (*Ursinia calenduliflora*), and yellow duikerwortel, or pietsnot (*Grielum humifusum*), in the foreground. The gifbos (*Euphorbia mauritanica*), a rapid-growing pioneer plant, has finger-like succulent stems. The sand olive (*Dodonea viscosa* subsp. *angustifolia*) – seen in the background – is widepread throughout the Hardeveld.

LEFT Meidestert (*Lapeirousia silenoides*), a strikingly attractive member of the iris family (Iridaceae), is common on Namaqualand's granite outcrops. Restricted to the semi-arid winter-rainfall Cape region, it sheds its foliage and 'disappears' underground with the onset of the dry summer months, its bell-shaped corms storing sufficient moisture to carry it through the summer resting period.

OPPOSITE The pienkaandblom (*Hesperantha pauciflora*) and sambreeltjies (*Felicia* sp.) in flower at Niewoudtville – a bulb hot-spot that probably houses the richest diversity of bulbs in the world – on the Bokkeveld Escarpment.

Introducing Gerhard Dreyer's Wild Flowers

Botterboom (*Tylecodon paniculatus*), strandvygie (*Ruschia macowanii*), soetkopdikblaar (*Senecio sarcoides*), steenbokmelkbos (*Euphorbia burmannii*) and yellow vierkantgombos (*Oedera uniflora*) at Yzerfontein.

S outh Africa is well known for its mineral wealth, but its true 'gold' lies in its rich and incomparable plant diversity. More than half the country's plant species are endemic to the subregion, and much of South Africa's flora is unique to the country.

A number of South Africa's plants have extraordinarily attractive ornamental features, and, because they are so adaptable and easy to grow, many of these have become the world's most popular house and garden plants. Among others, geraniums (*Pelargonium*), spider plants (*Cholorphytum comosum*), bokbaaivygies, or Livingstone daisies (*Dorotheanthus bellidiformis*), Barberton daisies (*Gerbera*), clivias (*Clivia*) and birds-of-paradise (*Strelitzia*), are grown throughout the world.

And, South Africa's bulb and succulent plant wealth surpasses that of any region on earth. Almost half of the world's bulb species originate from the winter-rainfall Cape region, and the succulent plant diversity of the Western and Northern Cape provinces is unequalled.

Water-katstert (*Bulbinella nutans*) in flower at Niewoudtville during spring. This is one of 14 *Bulbinella* species found in the Cape region; it is distributed eastwards to the Swellendam district of the Western Cape.

It is said that more money is made on the world market selling flowers of South African origin than the total value of the country's annual gold production. If you consider that Europe's total floral species number about 10 000, and that the much smaller South African region hosts some 23 000 species altogether, it isn't difficult to believe.

South African flora is further enriched by the two floral kingdoms that lie within its borders: the Cape Floral Kingdom, which is confined to the south-western winter-rainfall region, and the central-northern savanna, grassland, thicket and smaller forest patches that together make up the Palaeotropical Kingdom. In the latter regions, the climate is warm and subtropical, although winters are cooler. The climate of the Cape is mild (warm-temperate) and influenced by the cold, north-flowing Benguela Current of the Atlantic Ocean. Here the growing season coincides with the region's winter rainfall.

Recently, the Cape Floral Kingdom was singled out from 25 world ecological hot-spot areas as being of 'irreplaceable value'. This is not surprising, as the Kingdom hosts some 8 500 species, of which two-thirds are endemic.

Between these two wonders of nature lies the Karoo, a seemingly desolate, semi-arid stretch of land that is enriched by flora of both the kingdoms that flank it.

South Africa's rich floristic diversity reflects variety in climate and terrain, and a long history of isolation in the south-western corner of the African continent.

The topographical lay of the land is at once characterised by the interior Great Escarpment, a grassy plateau (with a mean altitude of 1 200 metres above sea level), which is separated from the sea by a narrow coastal strip.

The mighty Drakensberg range that fringes the plateau attains its peak (at about 3 000 metres) in the east, at the Lesotho-South Africa border. The escarpment slopes off to the north and

The striking yellow duikerwortel or pietsnot (*Grielum humifusum*), grows wild between orange Namaqualand daisies (*Dimorphoteca sinuata*) and purplish sambreeltjies (*Felicia* sp.) in the spring months in Namaqualand.

south, and tilts slightly towards the west, at an altitude of about 800 to 1 000 metres.

The climate on the plateau and in the higher reaches of the escarpment is cold, with occasional snow and frost during winter. Vegetation here consists mainly of grassland, with the occasional shrubs or small trees in protected rocky sites.

To the south of the Great Escarpment, and running right down to the coast and then parallel to it, is a continuous range known as the Cape Fold Mountains. Here, in these mineral-poor soils and among quartzitic rock, fynbos vegetation can be found. In the south-eastern reaches of the belt that makes up the Cape Fold Mountains, rainfall is high and perennial, and it is here that the Knysna forest – with it magnificent giant yellowwood trees (*Podocarpus falcatus*) – stretches along the coast.

Two-thirds of South Africa is subject to an annual rainfall of less than 500 millimetres, and the bulk of this area comprises semi-desert Karoo vegetation. The western extreme and the south-western reaches of this semi-desert region receive cyclonic rainfall, mainly during winter, and here the vegetation consists of what are known as succulent Karoo plants.

Rat's-tail (*Babiana ringens*) is conspicuous on the coastal dunes at Lambertsbaai in September. The red, tubular flowers are pollinated by sunbirds. Yellow-flowered duin-gousblom (*Didelta carnosa* var. *tomentosa*) are typically found among the pink-purple strandvygie (*Ruschia macowanii*) at Lambertsbaai.

The sandlelie (*Babiana plicata*) can be found in coastal dune bush in Namaqualand. Its flowers are irresistable to dusky, malachite and lesser double-collared sunbirds, which act as pollinators for the plant.

The northern reaches of the country (Kalahari and Bushveld) are, in part, mountainous, dissected by river valleys and comprising vast plains with bushveld vegetation such as thorn trees (*Acacia*), marulas (*Sclerocarya*), bushwillows (*Combretum*) and magestic baobabs (*Adansonia digitata*). Here, rain falls mainly during the spring and summer months.

Between the respective summer- and winter-rainfall regions lies an area of transition, in which rain may fall at any time of the year – and in some years, not at all.

South Africa's plant species are not only visually appealing, but they represent some of the world's most peculiar life forms and adaptations, and specific shapes, sizes and growth patterns reflect individual interactions with the environment. And, within each vegetation type, plants are shaped further by factors such fire, grazing and frost. For example, fynbos and grasslands have become so adapted to fire that the vegetation deteriorates without it. Within the fynbos, many protea species retain the seeds held in their flower heads, only releasing them after a fire, and many seeds, in fact, require the smoke of a fire before they can successfully germinate. Other plant species have persistent rootstocks or bulbs, from which they only resprout after a fire.

The 40 or more stone-plant (*Lithops*) species are all endemic to southern Africa. Pofadder beesklou (*L. dorothea*) (above), found near Pofadder, grows in reddish, weathered, granite soil in Bushmanland in the Northern Cape.

Katnaels (*Hyobanche sanguinea*), resembling cat's nails, and also known as aardroos, rooipop, or soetpop, is a root parasite, which only becomes conspicuous when it is in flower (winter to spring). It is one of seven southern African *Hyobanche* species, and is widespread in sandy regions.

Geeltjienkerientjee (*Ornithogalum dubium*), a bulbous plant found in the Western and Eastern Cape regions, one of about 60 South African *Ornithogalum* species. Its colour is variable.

Many bulbous species, including fire lilies (*Cyrtanthus, Nerine*) flower profusely after a fire. Wagon trees (*Protea nidita*) and klipkershout (*Maytenus oleoides*) each sport a thick, corky bark, which protects them during fire.

In the southern and western Karoo regions, vegetation is sparse, and summers are extremely dry and hot. It is here where the world's highest concentration of bulbous and succulent plants occurs. Succulents conserve water in their fleshy leaves, stems or roots, while bulbs harvest sunlight through their green leaves, and manufacture food from water, mineral and carbon dioxide resources, storing and protecting their 'investment' below soil level. Bulbs disappear for the 'resting' season, only to re-emerge during the onset of rains, when the entire process starts again.

The fleshy nature of succulents makes them an attractive food source for Karoo wildlife. However, some species, such as spekboom, ox-tongue and members of the stonecrop family (Crassulaceae), have become adapted to grazing, and, indeed, take advantage of the abuse. For example, the branch of a spekboom broken off by elephant will simply re-root on the ground where it has fallen. Similarly, partly grazed leaf fragments of ox-tongue (*Gasteria*) and kerkei (*Crassula ovata*) will regenerate, where they have fallen, when the dassies or tortoises move on. Stone plants (*Lithops, Pleiospilos*) mirror the surrounding stones or pebbles, and thus escape predation by camouflage. The sap of the conspicuous krantz aloe (*Aloe arborescens*) as well as that of the Cape bitter aloe (*A. ferox*), makes grazing a bitter experience, and many other succulent species are armed with spines or thorns to deter prospective predators.

Namaqualand and the Western Cape's annuals, which burst into spectacular bloom in the spring months, escape the dry conditions by 'hiding' in their seed stage during the long summer months, and germinating only when conditions are favourable in autumn. At the end of their short lifespan, their seeds are again dispersed, and the cycle begins anew.

The winter-rainfall Cape flora consists mainly of fynbos and succulent Karoo species.

The krantz aloe (*Aloe arborescens*), an arborescent, shrubby plant, has a widespread distribution from the Western Cape to Malawi in the north. It is widely grown in suburban gardens, and flowers during winter.

The tubular flowers of the halfmens (*Pachypodium namaquanum*). Endemic to the mountainous desert area of the Richtersveld and the lower Orange River Valley, the halfmens is a sparingly branched succulent-stemmed tree, which reaches heights of up to 2.5 metres.

The cigarette mesemb (*Cheiridopsis cigarettifera*) a small, cluster-forming spring-flowering succulent plant found on dry gravel slopes, is widespread in the semi-arid, winter-rainfall succulent Karoo region.

Plants that make up the fynbos biome have developed survival characteristics such as long-lived, firm, leathery leaves (often narrow) that are covered with a waxy skin or epidermis. Of course, fynbos plants are poor in nutrients, and are therefore unattractive to animals anyway.

Fynbos is confined to mineral-poor, acidic, sandy soils derived from the quartzitic sandstone rocks of the Cape Fold Mountains, and its species are accustomed to the area's dry summer conditions and soil deficiencies.

Nonetheless, fynbos is renowned for its species richness, and comprises various prominent botanical families, specifically, proteas (Proteaceae), ericas (Ericaceae) and reeds (Restionaceae), but including buchu (Rutaceae). Everlastings (Helichryssum), and bulbs (*Zantedeschia*, *Gladiolus*, Watsonia, *Cyrtanthus* and *Ornithogalum*) are also very well represented.

Fynbos consists of evergreen shrublands, punctuated by larger shrubs and small trees. The shrublands consist, too, of many small, shrubby species such as ericas, but probably the most prominent species are the restios, or grass-like reeds. The collective fynbos species found in the richer, clay soils of the Cape – attractive bulb species are prolific in these soils – is termed renosterbos, because of the prominence of the pioneer shrub of the same name (*Elytropappus rhinocerotis*).

Along South Africa's West coast, the strandveld holds a variety of succulents, as well as bulbous plants interspersed with restios and taaibos (*Rhus*) shrubs.

But the succulent Karoo region, to which almost 80 per cent of the world's mesemb species are confined, is the jewel in the crown of the Cape Floral Kingdom. Namaqualand and the Little Karoo are especially rich in vygie (Mesembryanthemaceae) and stonecrop (Crassulaceae) species. These families are the life of the shrublands that burst into colourful array during spring, providing an unforgettable spectacle of flowering Namaqualand daisies and mesembs.

The succulent Karoo's paltry rainfall measures between 25 and 400 millimetres a year, and falls mainly from autumn to early spring, although additional moisture may be attributed to heavy coastal fog.

Many succulent plants have 'dwarf' characteristics, where their compact, 'alpine-like' growth forms hug the ground so that they may benefit from the thermal energy of the rock or soil. Most bulb species 'shut down' during the hot summer months, and *Conophytum*, *Cheiridopsis*, *Antimima* and *Sceletium* are protected by the dry leaf remains of the previous growing season.

The magnificent floral wealth captured in these pages reflects a pristine environment that requires sustained protection and proper management if it is to survive. Fortunately, in spite of urban expansion, more and more land has been set aside for conservation, and there is an increased awareness of future dependence on this valuable asset. South Africa's flora must be treated as a permanent, long-term investment, and the seeds of indigenous plant conservation must continue to be sowed so that the children of the future can reap its benefits.

The sand- or bloupypie (*Gladiolus gracilis*) 'sword lily' is found in renosterveld vegetation on lower, seasonally moist depressions and slopes from Piketberg to Albertinia, and is pollinated by the honeybee.

Spring-flowering orange Namaqualand daisy, or jakkalsblom (*Dimorphotheca sinuata*) and blue sambreel-astertjie (*Felicia australis*) are commonly found in the Western Cape and Namaqualand.

Left The rooipypie, also known as a red afrikaner, or suikerkan (*Gladiolus priorii*), grows on gravelly slopes in fynbos and renosterveld, and is endemic to the Western Cape. The spectacular 'sword lily' flowers during midwinter, and occasionally in autumn, when it is pollinated by sunbrids. It is one of about 100 *Gladiolus* species confined to the winter-rainfall Cape Flora.

Above April fools, also known as skeerkwas or strandveld poeierkwas (*Haemanthus pubescens*), from the coastal strandveld region of the Western Cape, is one of 23 indigenous *Haemanthus* species. These are bulbous plants with fleshy berries, and the genus belongs to the Amaryllidaceae plant family. Their characteristic inflorescences are reminiscent of a powder brush. The April fool's conspicuous red flowers appear during autumn, just before it sprouts its two strap-shaped hairy leaves.

Opposite The rooi-afrikaner (*Gladiolus watsonius*), from renosterveld regions in the Swartland, flowers during winter and spring. Note the conspicuously long, tubular flowers which are pollinated by sunbirds.

ABOVE The geel-afrikaner (*Gladiolus tristis*) (also known as aandblom or pypie), is widespread, and is found in seasonally marshy areas from Niewoudtville in the north (Western Cape) to Port Elizabeth in the east (Eastern Cape). Its flowers, which open late in the spring day, are heavily scented.

ABOVE The geurbobbejaantjie (*Babiana odorata*), a low-growing bulbous plant that flowers during spring, is found in the renosterveld regions of the Swartland (Western Cape). It is one of about 50 *Babiana* species that occur in the Cape region. The name 'bobbejaantjie' is derived from the Afrikaans for 'little baboon'.

ABOVE The kalkoentjie (_Gladiolus alatus_), is found in the Western and Northern Cape regions. Its flowers are sweetly scented. Note the curved stamens, which provide an inviting and convenient 'landing pad' for its bee (_Anthophora diversipes_) pollinator; the reward – sweet nectar, in exchange, of course, for pollination.

ABOVE The bokkeveldbontrokkie (_Hesperantha cucculata_), as its name implies, is found in the Bokkeveld region of the Western Cape. Another spring-flowering plant, it is one of 34 winter-rainfall Cape _Hesperantha_ species.

ABOVE The conspicuous geeluintjie (*Moraea neglecta*) from the Bokkeveld Mountains in the Western Cape. It is one of about 120 Cape *Moraea* species that belong to the iris family (Iridaceae).

ABOVE RIGHT Orange kalossies (*Ixia dubia*) are confined to the winter-rainfall regions of the Western Cape.

OPPOSITE The harlekynaandblom (*Hesperantha vaginata*) is found in the Cape's winter-rainfall regions in renosterveld and succulent Karoo vegetation, from the Bokkeveld to Calvinia. Some 30 aandblom (*Hesperantha*) species occur here.

OPPOSITE The Afrikaans name kelkiewyn (*Geissorhiza mathewsii*) for this striking 'satin flower', pertains to the shape of the flower, which resembles a winecup filled with red wine. This species is restricted to the Darling region of the Western Cape, and while it adds to the springtime spectacle of Darling's annual wild flower show, it can also be grown in containers.

ABOVE One of the most striking of South Africa's indigenous bulbs belongs to the genus *Geissorhiza*, appropriately known as satin flowers. The witring-kelkiewyn (*Geissorhiza radians*), which occurs in renosterveld from near Darling to Gordons Bay, flowers during the spring.

RIGHT The bleekogie-kelkiewyn, or bleeksysie (*Geissorhiza monanthos*), too, belongs to the 'satin flower' genus, and is found in the Swartland and surrounds.

LEFT The three-flowered pagoda, or Outeniekwa-stompie (*Mimetes pauciflorus*) reaches a height of two to three metres, and is, as its name suggests, restricted to fynbos regions of the Outeniqua Mountains of the Western and Eastern Cape. This shrub is one of 13 known *Mimetes* species (Protea) that is confined to fynbos.

ABOVE One of the members of the genus *Babiana* known locally as a geelbobbejaantjie (*Babiana pygmaea*); baboons have developed a taste for these fleshy corms.

OPPOSITE LEFT The shield-orchid, or moederkappie (*Ceratandra grandiflora*) occurs from the Gouritz River in the Western Cape, to Grahamstown in the Eastern Cape. It is one of only six *Ceratandra* species of orchid restricted to the Cape flora.

OPPOSITE RIGHT The opslagplakkie (*Crassula dichotoma*), flowering during spring. It is an occasionally encountered annual species from strandveld regions from Namaqualand to the Agulhas Plain.

LEFT AND BELOW Chinkerinchee (*Ornithogalum thyrsoides*) plants vary in size (20 to 80 centimetres tall), and commonly occur in fynbos, renosterveld and strandveld regions, often in dense stands that are conspicuous during spring. The bulb is a popular garden plant, and is cultivated worldwide. There are 120 different *Ornithogalum* species in the world, of which the greatest diversity is restricted to the Cape region.

OPPOSITE The rooikanol, or koffiepit (*Wachendorfia paniculata*) is widespread from the Bokkeveld escarpment in the Northern Cape, to Port Elizabeth in the Eastern Cape. Also a bulb, it belongs to the butterfly lily family (Haemodoraceae), and the characteristic red fleshy rootstock earned it its Afrikaans name ('rooi' = red). *Wachendorfia* is a small genus comprising only four species, and it is restricted to the winter-rainfall regions of South Africa.

ABOVE The klokkie-viooltjie (*Lachenalia hirta* var. *hirta*) occurs in sandy regions from Malmesbury to Namaqualand, in renosterveld and succulent Karoo vegetation. This popular bulb lies dormant during the Cape's long, dry summers.

ABOVE The renosterveld viooltjie (*Lachenalia longibracteata*) is confined to renosterveld regions, and can be found from Malmesbury to Vredenburg in the Western Cape. In the northern reaches of its distribution, this attractive bulb occurs on rocky outcrops.

ABOVE (LEFT AND RIGHT) The leaves of the vrat-viooltjie (*Lachenalia pustulata*), which occurs on the Cape's West Coast from the Peninsula to St Helena Bay, are characteristically marked with raised blemishes, hence its Afrikaans common name ('vrat' = 'pustule').

LEFT The large pink Afrikaner, or sandveldlelie (*Gladiolus caryophyllaceus*), flowers during autumn, and is probably pollinated by the long-tongued anthophorid bees. It occurs in dry fynbos regions, from southern Namaqualand to the lower slopes of the Groot Swartberg range in the east.

ABOVE Rooibobbejaantjie, or kelkiewyn (*Babiana rubrocyanea*), has striking red-and-blue flowers. The bulbous plant is pollinated by monkey-beetles and confined to the Darling area of the Western Cape.

OPPOSITE The uiltjie (*Moraea villosa* subsp. *villosa*) is one of the most attractive of the Western Cape's *Moraea* species. The plant thrives, mainly in renosterveld vegetation, from Gordons Bay to Ceres and Piketberg, and is easily cultivated.

PREVIOUS PAGE LEFT Dense stands of maartblom (*Brunsvigia bosmaniae*), which flowers during the autumn months. Typically found near rocky outcrops, it is widely distributed from Tygerberg in the south to the Bokkeveld Plateau in the north, occurring mainly in renosterveld and succulent Karoo regions.

PREVIOUS PAGE RIGHT Widespread Namaqualand daisies (*Dimorphotheca sinutata*) and soetgousblomme (*Arctotheca calendula*) occur side by side in the Western and Northern Cape.

LEFT The waterkatstert (*Bulbinella nutans*) in flower during spring. As the Afrikaans name suggests, this bulb is found in moist habitats, and it occurs in vleis and moist depressions along the Bokkeveld escarpment.

BELOW The yellow frutang (*Romulea flava*) is a small, winter-spring flowering bulb, which occurs in fynbos and renosterveld of the Western Cape. The approximately 65 *Romulea* species are confined to the winter-rainfall region of South Africa. Dormant during summer, these small plants thrive in containers.

OPPOSITE The duikerwortel (*Grielum humifusum*) and the blou-uintjie (*Moraea tripetala*) flower simultaneously in spring at Tweeriviere, Namaqualand.

LEFT AND ABOVE The blou-afrikaner or sandpypie (*Gladiolus carinatus*) is widespread in dry fynbos regions from the Bokkeveld escarpment in the west to Knysna in the east. It is pollinated by the honeybee (*Apis mellifera*) and long-tongued Anthophoridae bees.

OPPOSITE The bright red, sweetly scented flowers of the kalkoentjie (*Gladiolus alatus*) – commonly found in dry fynbos, renosterveld and strandveld – are pollinated by *Anthophora diversipes* bees.

PREVIOUS PAGE LEFT Flowering orange berggousblom (*Ursinia calenduliflora*), purple sporrie (*Heliophila coronopifolia*), and yellow hongerblom (*Senecio cardaminifolius*) are interspersed with sweet-thorn (*Acacia karroo*) trees at Skilpad Wildflower Reserve, now part of the Namaqua National Park.

PREVIOUS PAGE RIGHT Spring annuals at Garies, in the heart of Namaqualand: yellow teebossie (*Leysera tenella*), orange Namaqualand daisy (*Dimorphotheca sinuata*) and spreading yellow-flowering gifmelkbos (*Euphorbia mauritanica*) shrub, and bergvygie (*Lampranthus hoerleianus*) – in the foreground on the right.

LEFT Bergbobbejaantjie (*Babiana framesii*) is found from Niewoudtville to Namaqualand in rocky habitats, and is one of about 50 *Babiana* species that is confined to the winter-rainfall Cape Flora.

ABOVE Spring-flowering persbobbejaantjies (*Babiana angustifolia*), pollinated mainly by solitary bees (*Anthophora diversipes*), are widespread in the clay soils of the Swartland in the Western Cape.

OPPOSITE The pronkbobbejaantjie (*Babiana sambucina*) flowers during winter and spring, and can be found in fynbos vegetation from the Bokkeveld escarpment near Niewoudtville in the west, to Port Elizabeth in the east.

ABOVE The blou spinnekopblom (*Ferraria uncinata*), found in succulent Karoo and renosterveld from Namaqualand (Northern Cape) to Kalbaskraal (Western Cape) in the south, flowers during spring.

ABOVE RIGHT The widespread vlei-aandblom, or trompetter (*Gladiolus tristis*), occurs in marshy depressions in fynbos and renosterveld in the Northern, Western and Eastern Cape.

OPPOSITE LEFT The flower of the groenkalkoentjie (*Gladiolus orchidiflorus*) resembles an orchid, hence its specific botanical name, *orchidiflorus*. It is a heavily scented, spring-flowering plant, and pollinated by Anthophoridae and Apidae bees. It is widely distributed, occurring in fynbos, succulent Karoo, Nama Karoo and Grassland habitats. It is also found in the the Free State and parts of Namibia.

OPPOSITE RIGHT *Gladiolus* species are found in most habitats from the southern tip of Africa at Cape Agulhas, to the highest peaks along the Drakensberg escarpment. Worldwide, there are 250 sword lily species, and 163 occur in South Africa, mostly in the winter-rainfall regions, their habitats ranging from sandy flats to sheer cliff faces. Many are pollinated by long-tongued Anthophoridae bees.

LEFT Spring-flowering donkerogies (*Moraea gigandra*) occur in renosterveld in the Swartland (Western Cape).

BELOW The grysastertjie (*Amellus tenuifolius*), a spreading perennial, bears grey, silky hairs – for which it is named. The hairs protect the inner tissue from excessive sunlight, and, as a result help the plant to conserve water. It is widespread on sandy soils in strandveld near the coast.

OPPOSITE The rooigousblom (*Gazania rigida*) is commonly found from southern Namibia and Namaqualand, to Humansdorp in the Eastern Cape. Here it is pictured among blue sambreelastertjies (*Felicia australis*), botterblomfroetangs (*Romulea diversiformis*) and pienkaandblomme (*Hesperantha pauciflora*).

ABOVE Sporrie, or blueflax (*Heliophila coronopifolia*) is a common annual.

ABOVE RIGHT The water phlox, or vleiblommetjie (*Onixotis stricta*) is an attractive, spring-flowering aquatic bulb found in seasonal pools and streams in the Cape.

OPPOSITE A close-up of the water phlox or vleiblommetjie (*Onixotis stricta*). The plant belongs to the Colchicaceae family, and is pollinated by honeybees (*Apis mellifera*). It grows up to 50 centimetres in height, and when the pools in which the plant grows dry up during summer, the plant becomes deciduous.

ABOVE The cigarette mesemb (*Cheiridopsis cigarettifera*), a small cluster-forming, spring-flowering plant found on dry gravel slopes, is widespead in the succulent Karoo region. The plant is so-named because the fused leaf pair and remnants of the previous year's leaves resemble a cigarette. In fact, they use the desiccated old leaf pair as a cover, to protect the developing new young growth. It is one of 34 *Cheiridopsis* species endemic to the winter-rainfall semi-arid regions of the Western and Northern Cape.

TOP RIGHT The sorrel genus comprises about 500 species worldwide. *Oxalis* species are effective drought evaders; they have a short growth cycle during the cool winter and spring months, then disappear underground for the long dry summer. This yellow sorrel (*Oxalis namaquana*) occurs at Garies.

RIGHT A geeltjienkerientjee (*Ornithogalum dubium*), from the southern and eastern Cape. It grows in dry fynbos, succulent Karoo and renosterveld, flowering from spring to early summer.

OPPOSITE Pietsnot, or duikerwortel (*Grielum humifusum*) sambreeltjies (*Felicia australis*), Namaqualand daisies (*Dimorphotheca sinuata*) and yellow hongerblom (*Senecio cardaminifolius*), each vividly coloured to attract pollinators and maximise propagation during their brief spring floral peak.

PREVIOUS PAGE LEFT Disturbed soil stimulates the germination of Namaqua annuals during late autumn, reacting in a mass display of orange Namaqualand daisies (*Dimorphotheca sinuata*) and yellow hongerblom (*Senecio cardaminifolius*) at Kamieskroon. Annuals are effective drought evaders; they remain dormant as seeds during the long, dry summers, only to germinate after the first good autumn rains.

PREVIOUS PAGE RIGHT Shrubby peperbos (*Montinia caryophyllacea*) patches flounder in a sea of yellow hongerblom (*Senecio cardaminifolius*), orange botterblom (*Gazania krebsiana*), white raindaisy (*Dimorphotheca pluvialis*) and purple douvygie (*Drosanthemum hispidum*).

LEFT A natural granite rock garden comes to life during spring. The rock crevices provide an effective hiding place for fleshy bulbous storage organs during summer. Here meidestert, or koringblommetjie (*Laperouisia silenoides*), viooltjie (*Lachenalia carnosa*), and blougif (*Bulbine praemorsa*) are in full flower.

BELOW The Liliputian world of the Knersvlakte is extremely rich in dwarf succulents. The structure of each species reflects its individual adaptation to local conditions. Buttons (*Conophytum pearsonii* var. *mintutum*) flower at the end of their resting season (autumn), attracting long-proboscid flies. Note that the succulent plant bodies are covered with the protective leaf remnants of the previous season's growth. The white reflects the sun, and minimises heat absorbtion during summer. The plant's low, tufted 'alpine' growth maximises heat absorption during the short, cool winter days.

OPPOSITE A natural rock garden of purplish-pink viooltjies (*Lachenalia carnosa*), koringblommetjies (*Lapeirousia silenoides*) and yellow knoppies (*Cotula microglossa*) in the Richtersveld, Northern Cape.

ABOVE The jakkalskos (*Harveya squamosa*), is an effective root parasite, which only shows its 'face' during its floral display in an effort to attract pollinators; it 'steals' moisture and nourishment from adjacent plant species, such as the *Othonna* daisy, by attaching its roots to the host plant.

ABOVE The very striking yellow form of the sandui, or 'lemon flame' (*Veltheimia bracteata*). The orange form, which is frequently cultivated, is common in the Eastern Cape. It has a rosette of attractive, dark green, spreading, tongue-shaped leaves, and grows among thickets and coastal forests in well-drained regions.

Above The geelkappie (*Eulophia speciosa*) is a terrestrial evergreen orchid found in the eastern coastal regions of the Western and Eastern Cape. The *Eulophia*'s thick, leathery leaves and shallow, spreading, spongy roots maximise effective moisture retention. There are about 40 indigenous *Eulophia* species in South Africa.

Above The katstert (*Bulbinella latifolia* var. *doleritica*) represent one of many of the Bokkeveld's endemic plant species. This variety grows in dolerite soils near Niewoudtville. This is one of 23 *Bulbinella* species that occur in South Africa and in New Zealand.

PREVIOUS PAGES A typical spring-time strandveld scene at Postberg on the Cape's West Coast, with common white rain daisy (*Dimorphotheca pluvialis*), sporrie, or blueflax (*Heliophila coronopifolia*), yellow buttons (*Cotula duckittiae*), shrubby sandbobbejaankool (*Othonna coronopifolia*), and orange lemoenvygie (*Lampranthus aureus*).

LEFT The beautiful knikkertjie, or froetang (*Romulea rosea*) thrives in containers, and is a common sight on the Bokkeveld Escarpment at springtime. It is pollinated by honeybees (*Apis mellifera*).

ABOVE The beautiful snotrosie (*Drosera cistiflora*) grows in wet areas in mineral-poor, acid, sandy soils deprived of nitrogen, alongside annuals such as purple sporrie (*Heliophila coronopifolia*). The leaves of the *Drosera* species are covered in glands that secrete a sticky substance that at once attracts and traps small insects, dissolving the bug so that the plant can absorb its nutrients.

OPPOSITE Darling froetang (*Romulea eximia*) and witring-kelkiewyn (*Geissorhiza radians*).

LEFT A spring-flowering bulb, the hairy sandveldbobbejaantjie (*Babiana nana*) grows in the Swartland (from Piketberg to Cape Town), in renosterveld habitat. It is one of approximately 65 species that belong to the genus *Babiana* (family Iridaceae)

ABOVE Another attractive bobbejaantjie from the Western Cape winter-rainfall region, *Babiana ambigua* is distributed from Klawer in the north to Riversdale in the east. *Babiana* belongs to the Iris family, the largest of South Africa's bulb families, of which about 650 species occur in the winter-rainfall Cape flora.

ABOVE The *Geissorhiza aspera* satin flower is pollinated by bees. It widespread from the Gifberg to Bredasdorp, and grows in sandy soil in fynbos habitat. There are about 80 *Geissorhiza* species confined to the winter-rainfall Western Cape region. They are deciduous plants, and flowers sprout annually in summer from their fleshy, rounded corms.

LEFT The Nieuwoudtville sysie (*Geissorhiza splendidissima*) is one of the many bulbous plants that are confined to renosterveld habitat in the Niewoudtville region of the Bokkeveld escarpment.

Previous page left The krantz aloe (*Aloe arborescens*) is commonly found in the coastal and mountainous regions of south-eastern and eastern South Africa. It is a rapid-growing 'bush', and the sap from its soft, fleshy leaves can be effectively used to soothe burns and other wounds.

Previous page right A member of the Protea (Proteaceae) family, the silver pagoda (*Mimetes argenteus*) is endemic to the quartzitic sandstone mountains of the Western Cape. Well adapted to the region's windy, dry summers, it reaches some 3.5 metres in height. The silver hairs that line its leaves block out excessive sunlight and minimise transpiration.

These pages The vleibobbejaantjie (*Babiana angustifolia*) (left), a Swartland endemic, occurs in renosterveld in seasonally moist depressions, while bergbobbejaantjies (*B. framesii*) (above) are found from Niewoudtville to Namaqualand in rocky habitats. A strikingly coloured rooibobbejaantjie (*B. rubrocyanea*) (opposite).

ABOVE The dark, fetid-smelling swartkoppie (*Wurmbea marginata*) is one of South Africa's 'carrion' flowers, specifically designed to attract flies for pollination. It occurs in renosterveld regions from Hopefield in the west, to Albertinia in the east (Western Cape).

ABOVE The Cape star, or geelpoublom (*Spiloxene canaliculata*) occurs in seasonally moist depressions in renosterveld habitat, from Darling to the Cape Peninsula. The dark centre of its flower is propably pollinated by monkey-beetles. After fruiting and during the dry summer months, the bulb lies dormant.

ABOVE Geelkoppies (*Ornithogalum suaveolens*) are widely distributed in the winter-rainfall Cape region, from Namaqualand to Humansdorp. This species, known locally as chinkerinchee (or tjienkerientjee, in Afrikaans), is one of about 60 *Ornithogalum* species found in South Africa.

ABOVE One of only two members of the *Veltheimia* genus, the sandlelie (*Veltheimia capensis*) bears aloe-like, orange-coloured flowers, its base a rosette of attractive grey-green, spreading tongue-shaped leaves, curled along their margins. The plant grows among rocks and boulders in succulent Karoo vegetation.

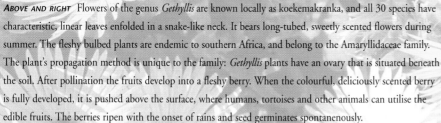

ABOVE AND RIGHT Flowers of the genus *Gethyllis* are known locally as koekemakranka, and all 30 species have characteristic, linear leaves enfolded in a snake-like neck. It bears long-tubed, sweetly scented flowers during summer. The fleshy bulbed plants are endemic to southern Africa, and belong to the Amaryllidaceae family. The plant's propagation method is unique to the family: *Gethyllis* plants have an ovary that is situated beneath the soil. After pollination the fruits develop into a fleshy berry. When the colourful, deliciously scented berry is fully developed, it is pushed above the surface, where humans, tortoises and other animals can utilise the edible fruits. The berries ripen with the onset of rains and seed germinates spontanenously.

TOP RIGHT Candelabra lilies (*Brunsvigia* spp.) are usually large, bulbous species, some with an inflorescence of up to 65 centimetres. The plant's four to six leaves usually lie flat on the ground, and their conspicuously colorful red, orange, pink or white flowers are carried in distinct rounded umbels that appear during autumn. There are about 10 *Brunsvigia* species in the winter-rainfall Cape region.

OPPOSITE The Gifberg, which is part of the Bokkeveld escarpment, houses many endemic plants, such as the Gifberg froetang (*Romulea sladenii*), which occurs in shallow rocky soil in dry fynbos habitat on top of the mountain of the same name, near Vanrhynsdorp, Western Cape.

PREVIOUS PAGES The disturbed soils of once-cultivated farmlands provide the perfect germinating grounds for dominant orange berggousblom (*Ursinia calenduliflora*) and forget-me-nots (*Anchusa capensis*), at Skilpad (Namaqua National Park).

ABOVE The botterblom (*Gazania krebsiana*) stands out among purple douvygie (*Drosanthemum hispidum*) at Goegap, near Springbok in the Northern Cape. Local tortoises – tent tortoise (*Psammobatus tentorius*), angulate tortoise (*Chesina angulata*), and speckled padloper (*Homopus signatus*) – are fond of the obviously tasty *Gazania* flowers.

TOP RIGHT The margriet (*Ursinia speciosa*) in flower at Biedouw Valley, Clanwilliam, Western Cape.

RIGHT The golden lampranthus or lemoenvygie (*Lampranthus aureus*), purple sporrie (*Heliophila coronopifolia*) and yellow kleinganskos (*Cotula barbata*) near the coast at Postberg (West Coast). The golden lampranthus is endemic to the West Coast.

OPPOSITE Livingstone daisies (*Dorotheanthus bellidiformis*) belong to the Mesembryanthemaceae family. These flowers, known locally as bokbaaivygies, are popular garden subjects throughout the world. There are six indigenous species, all of which are annuals and all endemic to the winter-rainfall Cape region. *D. bellidiformis* is widespread, especially in strandveld and coastal fynbos, and the flower colour is variable. The single orange flower is a Namaqualand daisy (*Dimorphotheca sinuata*).

LEFT The satin flower, or satynblom (*Romulea sabulosa*) from the Bokkeveld Mountains near Niewoudtville, occurs in renosterveld habitat.

BELOW The Outeniqua pincushion (*Leucospermum glabrum*) is also frequently cultivated for its ornamental flowers. Pincushions (*Leucospermum* spp.) are immediately recognisable by their many colourful protruding styles, which collectively resemble a pincushion. They are attractive members of the Protea family (Proteaceae).

OPPOSITE The wildestokroos (*Anisodontea malvastroides*) a shrub with small hibiscus-like (family Malvaceae) flowers, is common on the escparment mountains in the Nama Karoo (Northern Cape). These shrubs are sometimes cultivated.

OVERLEAF Flowering duikerwortel (*Grielum humifusum*), sambreeltjies (*Felicia australis*) and peperbos (*Montinia caryophyllacea*) in the Richtersveld, Northern Cape. The typical gravel farm roads in this region, where the road edges and the characteristic, 'central island' (known in Afrikaans as a 'middelmannetjie') are dotted with wild flowers.

Left Rooipypie (*Watsonia galpinii*) is an evergreen species from the Swartberg and Outeniqua mountains of the Western Cape. It flowers during summer and autumn, and is pollinated by sunbirds. Watsonias are popular garden subjects.

Above The striking harlequin flower, or fluweeltjie (*Sparaxis tricolor*) from the Bokkeveld escarpment near Niewoudtville in the Northern Cape.

Opposite The maartblom (*Brunsvigia marginata*) produces rounded umbels of brilliantly red, bell-shaped flowers in autumn, and is restricted to shale bands in renosterveld vegetation (Citrusdal to Du Toitskloof). Note the extended stamens, ready to release their pollen to visiting pollinators.

LEFT The ratstail (*Babiana ringens*) at Postberg on the West Coast. Their tubular, funnel-shaped flowers are produced close to the ground, and are pollinated by sunbirds. Ratstail is distributed on sandy plains in fynbos and strandveld, often near the coast from the Bokkeveld escarpment to Still Bay in the east (Western Cape).

BELOW Snotrosie (*Drosera cistiflora*) is widely distributed from Namaqualand (Northern Cape) to Port Elizabeth (Eastern Cape). It is confined to wet depressions, where it grows alongside wild cineraria (*Senecio elegans*).

OPPOSITE A close-up view of the snotrosie (*Drosera cistiflora*) flower. Note its hairy leaves and glands for trapping small insects. There are 20 *Drosera* species indigenous to South Africa, of which *D. regia* is the largest.

Left The well-known Namaqua koekemakranka (*Gethyllis namaquensis*). It is bulbous and summer deciduous, and its sweetly scented white to light pink flowers appear during November and December. The fruits of the flower are popular, and are often used to flavour brandy.

Above The spinnekopblom, also known as uiltjie, or inkpotjie (*Ferraria crispa*) has sword-shaped leaves. Its dark flowers are pollinated by flies. During winter, the corm 'rests', and in spring, the spinnekopblom flowers. It occurs in coastal regions, usually on sandstone and granite outcrops from Lamberts Bay to Mossel Bay. There are about 10 *Ferraria* species in the winter-rainfall Cape region of South Africa.

Opposite Geelbobbejaanboek (*Daubenia echinata* syn. *Neobakeria angustifolia*) is a low-growing, bulbous plant from the Bokkeveld escarpment (Northern Cape) to Saldanha (Western Cape). The plants are dormant during the dry summer season.

LEFT The klippypie (*Gladiolus hyalinus*) has a wide distribution, from Namaqualand to Port Alfred, in fynbos and renosterveld habitat. It flowers during winter and spring.

BELOW The March lily (*Amaryllis belladonna*) is propably the best known of the Cape bulbs, and their beautiful, trumpet-shaped flowers grace the land during the month of March – hence the common name. March lilies are commonly found in the Western Cape, from the Olifants River (near Citrusdal), to Knynsa, occurring in coastal fynbos, strandveld and renosterveld. The lily, which thrives in gardens, is easily grown from seed, and is one of only two species in the genus *Amaryllus*.

OPPOSITE The witbobbejaantjie (*Babiana tubulosa*) occurs naturally in strandveld and coastal fynbos, from Elands Bay in the north, to Riversdale in the east (Western Cape), although it can be grown as a pot plant. It is spring flowering, and favours sandy soil.

LEFT Gousblom (*Arctotis hirsuta*) has a wide distribution, and is common on the Cape Peninsula and northwards to Namaqualand. Favouring strandveld and coastal fynbos, it flowers profusely during spring. The gousblom is easy to grown in Western Cape coastal regions; seeds should be sown in autumn.

ABOVE The lemoenvygie (*Lampranthus aureus*) occurs in strandveld and coastal fynbos vegetation, and is found north of Darling to Saldanha. The colour of winter and spring flowers is very variable, and ranges from orange to yellow to white. It is easily grown in gardens, and can be propagated from seeds or cuttings.

ABOVE The volstruisvygie (*Cephalophyllum spongiosum*) (left) is one of the most attractive of the mesemb species, and is found from north of the Olifants River (Western Cape), to Kleinzee (Northern Cape). The plants, which occur in strandveld, have finger-like leaves and fairly large fruiting capsules; they open during heavy rainfall, using the kinetic engergy of the falling raindrops to disperse their seed. The capsules close again when it becomes dry. The vygie is easily grown from seeds or cuttings, but needs lots of sun. The duin-gousblom (*Didelta carnosa* var. *tomentosa*) (right) is also commonly found in strandveld vegetation.

RIGHT The botterblom (*Gazania krebsiana*) is variable in colour and occurs thoughout South Africa, but the most attractive form of this flower is found in the winter-rainfall Cape region. It is easily cultivated, and is popular in gardens throughout the world.

OVERLEAF A typical view of the south-eastern Knersvlakte, showing the Bokkeveld escarpment, near Leeustert, Western Cape. The vegetation is typical of the succulent Karoo, and here a lone specimen of the alien (from North and central America) acacia-like honey mesquite (*Prosopis glandulosa* var. *torreyana*) stands out among a spectacular display of flowering orange beetle daisy (*Gorteria diffusa* subsp. *diffusa*), orange thorn-seed daisy (*Osteospermum pinnatum*) – a flat-growing annual with spiny seeds – and yellow teebossie (*Senecio cardaminifolius*).

BIBLIOGRAPHY

Manning, J., Goldblatt, P., and Snijman, D. 2002. *The Colour Encyclopedia of Cape Bulbs*. Timber Press, Cambridge, UK.

Smith, C. A. 1966. *Common Names of South African Plants*. Botanical Survey Memoir no 35. Government Printer.

Manning, J., and Goldblatt, P. 1996. *West Coast. South African Wild Flower Guide 7*. Botanical Society of South Africa.

Manning, J. and Goldblatt, P. 1997. *Niewoudtville (Bokkeveld Plateau and Hantam). South African Wild Flower Guide 9*. Botanical Society of South Africa.

Mason, H., and Du Plessis, E. et al. 1972. *Western Cape Sandveld Flowers*. C. Struik, Cape Town.

Le Roux, A., and Schelpe, T. 1988. *Namaqualand. South African Wild Flower Guide 1*. Botanical Society of South Africa.

Goldblatt, P., and Manning, J. 2000. *Cape Plants, A Conspectus of the Cape Flora of South Africa. Strelitzia 9*. National Botanical Institute and Missouri Botanical Garden.

Goldblatt, P., and Manning, J. 1998. *Gladiolus in Southern Africa*. Fernwood Press. Cape Town.